To all the entrepreneurs and startup founders who have taken the leap of faith to pursue their dreams and bring their ideas to life.

To the investors, mentors, and support networks who have believed in and supported these entrepreneurs, helping them to turn their ideas into successful businesses.

To the countless hours spent brainstorming, iterating, and hustling, and the moments of triumph and failure that make up the startup journey.

May this book serve as a helpful guide and resource to navigate the complex and ever-evolving world of startup jargon, and may it inspire and empower entrepreneurs to continue pushing the boundaries and building innovative, impactful businesses.

Thank you for your dedication and passion for building a brighter future for us all.

Special Thanks to My Grandmother Late Mrs. Poonam Devi (Amma). You have shown me what it means to be fearless, to take risks, and to never give up on my dreams.

STARTUP JARGONS

GUIDE FOR NEWBIE ENTREPRENEURS

AKSHAY RAJ

Made with ♥ on the Notion Press Platform
www.notionpress.com

Contents

Foreword

The world of startups is one that is constantly evolving and changing. As the landscape of entrepreneurship continues to shift, so too does the language and jargon used within it. For entrepreneurs just starting out, this can make the process of building and growing a startup all the more daunting.

That's why this book is such a valuable resource. It provides a comprehensive guide to the world of startup jargon, breaking down complex concepts and terminology in a clear and concise manner. From "bootstrapping" to "unicorns," "lean startup" to "pitch deck," this book covers all of the key concepts and terms that are critical for success in the world of startups.

As an investor and mentor to startups, I've seen firsthand the importance of understanding startup jargon. It's not just about being able to communicate effectively with investors and other stakeholders; it's about having a deep understanding of the processes and strategies that are critical to building a successful startup.

Whether you're a first-time entrepreneur just starting out or a seasoned startup founder looking to refresh your knowledge, this book has something for you. With its clear and accessible language, it provides a wealth of information that will help you to navigate the world of startups with confidence and clarity.

I'm honored to have the opportunity to write the foreword for this book, and I hope that you find it to be a valuable resource on your own journey as an entrepreneur.

Best of luck on your startup journey!

-Akshay Raj

Preface

As an entrepreneur, you're no stranger to jargon. From "product-market fit" to "seed round," the language of startups is full of terms and concepts that can be difficult to understand, especially for those just starting out.

That's where this book comes in. Our goal with this guide is to demystify the world of startup jargon, breaking down key concepts and terminology in a way that is clear and easy to understand. Whether you're a first-time entrepreneur just starting out, or a seasoned startup founder looking to refresh your knowledge, this book has something for you.

Throughout the pages of this book, we cover a wide range of topics, from fundraising and pitching to product development and marketing. We've included definitions, explanations, and examples of all of the key terms and concepts you need to know, as well as tips and insights from experienced entrepreneurs and investors.

We know that the world of startups can be overwhelming, but we believe that with the right tools and knowledge, anyone can succeed. That's why we've created this guide - to help entrepreneurs like you navigate the complex and ever-evolving landscape of startup jargon.

We hope that you find this book to be a valuable resource as you build and grow your own startup. We're honored to be a part of your journey, and we wish you all the best as you work to bring your ideas to life.

Sincerely,

-Akshay Raj

Acknowledgements

Creating a guide like this is no small feat, and we couldn't have done it without the help and support of many people along the way. We'd like to take a moment to express our gratitude to all of those who have helped to make this book a reality.

First and foremost, we want to thank all of the entrepreneurs and startup founders who have inspired us with their creativity, dedication, and hard work. Your stories and experiences have provided the foundation for much of the content in this book.

We also want to thank the many investors, mentors, and support networks who have helped to guide and advise us over the years. Your wisdom and insight have been invaluable in shaping our understanding of the startup world.

To our colleagues and friends who have provided feedback and support throughout the writing process, thank you for your time, energy, and encouragement. Your contributions have helped to make this book stronger and more effective.

Finally, we want to thank our families for their love and support. Your patience and understanding throughout the long hours and late nights of writing and editing have been a constant source of motivation and inspiration.

We are honored and grateful to have had the opportunity to create this guide, and we hope that it serves as a helpful resource for entrepreneurs and startup founders for years to come.

Sincerely
Akshay Raj

Vaibhav Sharma

1

Funding and Investment

Funding and investment are essential components of any startup's growth and development. In this chapter, we'll cover the key terms and concepts related to startup funding and investment.

Angel Investor

An angel investor is an individual who provides funding for startups in exchange for an equity stake in the company. Angel investors are typically high-net-worth individuals who are interested in investing in early-stage companies with high growth potential. In addition to providing financial support, angel investors may also provide mentorship and guidance to the startup's founders.

Bootstrapping

Bootstrapping refers to starting a business without external funding or capital. This can be a challenging process, as the startup must rely solely on its own resources and revenue to finance its operations. However, bootstrapping can also give a startup greater control over its growth and development, as it is not beholden to the demands and expectations of outside investors.

Burn Rate

The burn rate is the rate at which a startup is spending its cash reserves to finance its operations. Burn rate is an important metric for investors, as it can indicate how quickly a startup is using up its cash and whether it will need additional funding to continue its growth.

Crowdfunding

Crowdfunding is the process of raising funds from a large number of people, typically through online platforms. Crowdfunding can be an effective way for startups to raise capital without giving up equity, and it can also help to generate buzz and publicity for the company.

Series A, B, C Funding

Series A, B, and C funding refer to rounds of funding that a startup goes through as it grows and scales. Each round typically involves raising larger amounts of capital from institutional investors such as venture capital firms or private equity funds. The terms of each round of funding can vary, but they often involve the startup giving up an equity stake in exchange for the investment.

Seed Funding

Seed funding refers to the initial capital raised to start a business, usually from family and friends or angel investors. Seed funding is typically used to develop a startup's initial product or service, build out its team, and begin generating revenue. Seed funding is often followed by additional rounds of funding as the startup grows and scales.

Understanding the world of funding and investment is essential for any startup founder or entrepreneur. By familiarizing yourself with these key terms and concepts, you'll be better equipped to navigate the complex landscape of startup financing and build a successful and sustainable business.

2

Business Development

Business development is the process of building and growing a startup's operations and revenue. In this chapter, we'll cover the key terms and concepts related to business development.

Business Model

A business model is a plan that outlines how a startup will generate revenue and make a profit. The business model should include a clear description of the startup's product or service, its target market, and its pricing strategy. A well-designed business model is essential for attracting investors and building a sustainable and profitable business.

Customer Acquisition Cost (CAC)

The customer acquisition cost is the cost of acquiring a new customer, including marketing and advertising expenses. CAC is an important metric for startups, as it can help to determine the viability and profitability of the business. By understanding the CAC, a startup can optimize its marketing and advertising strategy to minimize costs and maximize revenue.

Go-To-Market Strategy

The go-to-market strategy is the plan for how a startup will bring its product or service to market. This strategy should include a clear understanding of the target market, the marketing and advertising channels that will be used to reach customers, and the sales process. A well-designed go-to-market strategy can help to ensure that a startup's product or service is successful in the marketplace.

Minimum Viable Product (MVP)

The minimum viable product is the simplest version of a product or service that can be released to the market. The MVP should include the core features and functionality of the product or service, but it should also be simple enough to develop and launch quickly. The MVP can be used to validate the product or service concept, gather feedback from early customers, and iterate on the design and functionality.

Product-Market Fit

Product-market fit is the point at which a startup has identified a product that satisfies a real market need. This is a critical milestone for startups, as it indicates that the product or service has a viable market and can be successful in the long term. Achieving product-market fit often requires extensive market research and customer feedback, as well as ongoing iteration and development of the product or service.

Scalability

Scalability is the ability of a startup to grow its operations and revenue without a proportional increase in costs. Scalability is a key factor in the success of any startup, as it allows the company to grow rapidly and efficiently. To achieve scalability, a startup must have a well-designed business model, a strong go-to-market strategy, and a product or service that can be easily replicated and distributed.

Understanding the key concepts of business development is essential for any startup founder or entrepreneur. By familiarizing yourself with these terms, you'll be better equipped to build a successful and sustainable business that can grow and thrive in the long term.

3

Marketing and Sales

This Chapter focuses on the essential concepts and techniques of marketing and sales that are critical for the success of any startup. This chapter covers various aspects of marketing, including content marketing, conversion rates, lead generation, sales funnels, search engine optimization (SEO), and viral marketing.

Content Marketing: With the rise of digital channels and social media, content marketing has become an essential aspect of building a brand and attracting potential customers. It involves creating and sharing valuable and relevant content that can inform, educate, and engage a target audience. The content can come in various forms such as blog posts, videos, e-books, infographics, podcasts, and more.

Conversion Rate: The conversion rate measures the percentage of website visitors who take a desired action, such as making a purchase, filling out a form, or subscribing to a newsletter. It is an important metric for measuring the effectiveness of a business's marketing efforts. By tracking the conversion rate, businesses can identify areas for improvement in their marketing campaigns, website design, and user experience.

Lead Generation: Lead generation is the process of identifying and attracting potential customers to a business. It involves creating awareness and interest in a company's products or services and capturing contact information from potential customers. Lead generation can be done through various channels such as social media, email marketing, content marketing, search engine marketing, and more.

Sales Funnel: A sales funnel is the path that a potential customer takes from initial awareness of a product or service to making a purchase. It is typically divided into different stages such as awareness, interest, consideration, intent, and purchase. By understanding the different stages of the sales funnel, businesses can create targeted marketing and sales strategies to move potential customers through each stage and ultimately convert them into paying customers.

Search Engine Optimization (SEO): SEO is the process of optimizing a website's content and structure to improve its visibility and ranking on search engines like Google. By improving a website's ranking on search engines, businesses can increase their organic traffic and attract more potential customers. SEO involves various techniques such as keyword research, on-page optimization, link building, and more.

Viral Marketing: Viral marketing is a marketing technique that relies on word-of-mouth to spread a message or product to a large audience. It involves creating a unique and shareable message or product that people will want to share with their friends and family. By leveraging the power of social media and other digital channels, viral marketing can help businesses reach a large audience quickly and effectively. However, it can be challenging to create a viral campaign, and not all products or messages are suitable for viral marketing.

Branding: The process of creating a unique identity and image for a company, product, or service.

Call to Action (CTA): A prompt or instruction that encourages the audience to take a specific action, such as signing up for a newsletter or purchasing a product.

Growth Hacking: A marketing technique that focuses on rapidly and creatively experimenting with different marketing channels to identify the most effective ones.

4

Technology and Product Development

Technology and product development are critical aspects of building a successful startup. In this chapter, we explore key concepts related to the development and deployment of technology in startups, as well as product design and management.

Agile Development: Agile development is a software development methodology that emphasizes flexibility and rapid iteration. It involves cross-functional teams collaborating on small, incremental updates to a product or service, rather than long development cycles.

Artificial Intelligence (AI): Artificial intelligence is the simulation of human intelligence in machines. It includes processes such as learning, reasoning, and self-correction, and is used in a wide range of applications, from customer service chatbots to self-driving cars.

Beta Testing: Beta testing is the process of testing a product or service with a group of users before its official release. It allows startups to gather feedback and identify and fix issues before launching to a wider audience.

Cloud Computing: Cloud computing refers to the delivery of computing services, including storage and processing power, over the internet. It allows startups to access powerful computing resources without having to invest in expensive hardware.

Internet of Things (IoT): The Internet of Things is a network of physical devices, vehicles, and other items that are embedded with sensors, software, and connectivity. It allows for the collection and analysis of large amounts of data, which can be used to improve efficiency and create new products and services.

User Experience (UX): User experience refers to the overall experience that a user has when interacting with a product or service. It includes factors such as usability, accessibility, and design, and is critical to the success of any product or service.

API: Application Programming Interface, a set of protocols and tools for building software applications.

Backend: The part of a website or application that is responsible for storing and processing data.

Frontend: The part of a website or application that is visible to the user and interacts with the backend.

Open Source: Software that is freely available and can be modified and distributed by anyone.

Scalability: The ability of a website or application to handle increased traffic and usage without experiencing performance issues.

Stack: The set of software technologies used to build a website or application, including the programming languages, frameworks, and libraries.

By understanding and effectively utilizing these concepts, startups can build and deploy innovative and successful technology products and services.

5

Operations and Management

Burnout: A state of emotional, physical, and mental exhaustion caused by excessive and prolonged stress. Burnout can lead to decreased productivity, disengagement, and even physical health problems for both employees and founders.

Cash Flow: The movement of money in and out of a business, including revenue, expenses, and investments. Cash flow management is critical for startups to ensure they have enough cash on hand to cover expenses and fund growth.

Key Performance Indicators (KPIs): Specific metrics used to measure and evaluate the success of a business or project. KPIs can include financial metrics like revenue and profitability, as well as non-financial metrics like customer satisfaction and employee engagement.

Minimum Viable Team (MVT): The smallest team that can effectively develop and launch a product. Determining the MVT is important for startups to ensure they have the necessary resources and expertise to bring their product to market.

Pivot: A change in a company's business model or strategy in response to market feedback or changes. Pivoting can be a necessary step for startups to stay relevant and competitive in a rapidly changing market.

Runway: The amount of time that a startup has before it runs out of cash. Startups need to carefully manage their runway to ensure they can continue operating long enough to achieve profitability or secure additional funding.

Cash Burn Rate: The rate at which a startup is spending its available funds, often calculated as monthly expenses minus monthly revenue.

Efficiency: The ability of a business to maximize its use of resources to achieve its goals.

Management Team: The group of individuals responsible for overseeing the day-to-day operations and strategic direction of a business.

Milestones: Specific goals or achievements that a startup aims to reach in order to measure progress and success.

Operations: The processes and activities involved in running a business, including production, logistics, and customer service.

Productivity: The rate at which a business is able to produce goods or services, often measured by the amount of output per unit of input.

Supply Chain: The network of businesses and organizations involved in the production and delivery of a product or service.

6

Legal and Financial

This Chapter focuses on the legal and financial aspects of starting and running a business. Here are some key concepts discussed in this chapter:

Intellectual Property (IP): Intellectual property refers to the legal rights that protect creations of the mind, such as inventions, literary and artistic works, and symbols or designs. IP rights include patents, trademarks, copyrights, and trade secrets. Startups need to be aware of these rights and take steps to protect their intellectual property.

Initial Public Offering (IPO): An initial public offering is the first sale of a company's stock to the public. This is a significant milestone for startups as it provides access to public capital and raises the profile of the company. However, going public requires significant time and effort, as well as compliance with regulatory requirements.

Term Sheet: A term sheet is a non-binding document that outlines the key terms and conditions of a potential investment. It is typically used during the early stages of the fundraising process and provides a framework for negotiations between the startup and investors.

Vesting: Vesting is the process of earning equity in a company over time, often as an incentive for employees or founders. Vesting schedules typically require individuals to stay with the company for a certain period of time before they can fully own their equity.

Valuation: Valuation is the process of determining the value of a company, typically for investment or acquisition purposes. This is a critical factor in fundraising, as it helps investors assess the potential return on their investment.

Burnout: Burnout is a state of emotional, physical, and mental exhaustion caused by excessive and prolonged stress. This is a significant risk for startup founders and employees, who often work long hours under high-pressure conditions. It is important for startups to prioritize the well-being of their team members and take steps to prevent burnout.

7

People and Culture

Culture Fit: Refers to the extent to which an employee's values, personality, and work style align with those of the company's culture. A good culture fit is important for employee satisfaction and retention.

Diversity, Equity, and Inclusion (DEI): A set of practices aimed at creating a workplace that is diverse, equitable, and inclusive. This includes efforts to increase representation of underrepresented groups, eliminate bias in hiring and promotion, and create a welcoming and respectful environment for all employees.

Human Resources (HR): The department responsible for managing a company's employees. This includes recruitment, benefits administration, payroll, and ensuring compliance with employment laws and regulations.

Onboarding: The process of integrating a new employee into a company's culture and workflow. This includes orientation, training, and introductions to colleagues and the company's values and goals.

Remote Work: A work arrangement in which employees work from a location outside of the traditional office environment. Remote work has become increasingly common due to technological advances and the COVID-19 pandemic.

Talent Acquisition: The process of identifying, attracting, and hiring the best candidates for a job. This includes sourcing candidates through job postings, recruiting events, and referrals, as well as conducting interviews and making job offers.

8

Industry-Specific Jargon

Biotech: The application of biology and technology to create new products and technologies. Biotech is a field that combines biology and technology to develop new products and technologies.

EdTech refers to the use of technology to enhance and improve education.

FinTech involves the application of technology to financial services such as banking, investing, and insurance.

HealthTech utilizes technology to improve healthcare, including telemedicine and health data analytics.

PropTech uses technology to improve the real estate industry, including property management and smart building systems.

SaaS is a cloud-based software delivery model in which users pay a subscription fee for access to the software.

AdTech: The use of technology to deliver and manage digital advertising.

AgTech: The use of technology to improve agricultural processes and increase efficiency in farming.

CleanTech: The use of technology to reduce the environmental impact of human activities, such as renewable energy and sustainable transportation.

InsurTech: The application of technology to the insurance industry, including the use of artificial intelligence and machine learning to automate claims processing.

MarTech: The use of technology to support marketing activities, such as customer relationship management and data analytics.

RegTech: The use of technology to help companies comply with regulatory requirements and reporting obligations.

These industry-specific jargon terms are important for individuals working in these fields to understand and communicate effectively with colleagues and clients.

9

Incubation

Incubation is the process of nurturing startups and providing them with the resources they need to grow and succeed. This chapter explores the concept of incubation and the role of incubators in the startup ecosystem.

Incubators are organizations that provide support and resources to startups, typically in exchange for an equity stake in the company. These resources may include office space, mentorship, access to funding, and networking opportunities. Incubators are often run by universities, governments, or private companies.

The incubation process typically begins with the submission of an application by the startup. Once accepted, the startup will receive support and guidance from the incubator. This may include access to mentors who can provide advice and guidance, as well as office space and other resources.

Incubators can be a valuable resource for startups, particularly those that are just starting out. They can provide startups with access to funding and mentorship, which can help them to grow and succeed. However, it's important for startups to carefully evaluate potential incubators and choose one that is a good fit for their needs and goals.

Overall, incubation plays an important role in the startup ecosystem, providing startups with the resources and support they need to succeed.

Incubator: An organization or program that provides resources and support to early-stage startups, such as office space, mentorship, and funding.

Accelerator: Similar to an incubator, but with a more intensive focus on accelerating growth and development of a startup, often through a fixed-term program that includes mentorship, education, and networking opportunities.

Co-Working Space: Shared office space that allows individuals and small teams to work in a collaborative environment, often providing resources and amenities such as conference rooms, kitchen areas, and high-speed internet.

Demo Day: A culminating event at the end of an incubator or accelerator program where startups pitch their businesses to investors and other stakeholders.

Equity: Ownership in a company, often exchanged for investment capital.

Valuation: The estimated worth of a startup, often determined by factors such as revenue, market share, and growth potential.

Seed Fund: A type of venture capital fund that invests in early-stage startups, often during the seed round of funding.

10

Startup Valuation

Startup valuation is the process of estimating the value of a startup company. This is important for both investors and founders because it determines the equity share and worth of the company. Here are some key terms and concepts related to startup valuation:

Pre-Money Valuation: The value of a startup company before any new investment is made.

Post-Money Valuation: The value of a startup company after a new investment is made.

Dilution: The reduction in the percentage of ownership of existing shareholders as a result of new investment.

Equity: Ownership in a company, represented by shares.

Valuation Methods: There are several methods used to value a startup, including the Market Approach, Income Approach, and Asset Approach.

Comparable Analysis: A valuation method that compares a startup to similar companies that have recently been sold or have gone public.

Discounted Cash Flow (DCF): A valuation method that estimates the present value of future cash flows.

Burn Rate: The rate at which a startup is spending its cash reserves to finance its operations.

Revenue Multiple: A valuation method that multiples a startup's revenue by a certain factor to estimate its value.

Venture Capital Method: A valuation method that estimates the value of a startup based on the expected return on investment for venture capitalists.

Unicorn: A startup with a valuation of over $1 billion.

Decacorn: A startup with a valuation of over $10 billion.

Hectocorn: A startup with a valuation of over $100 billion.

Cockroach: A startup that prioritizes resilience and longevity over rapid growth and high valuation.

Lifestyle Business: A small business that prioritizes the owner's personal lifestyle and income over rapid growth or high valuation.

Niche Business: A business that focuses on a specific niche or market, rather than attempting to capture a broad audience.

Bootstrapped Business: A business that is built and funded without external investment or funding, often using the owner's personal savings and revenue generated by the business.

Understanding startup valuation is crucial for both founders and investors. By knowing the value of a startup, both parties can make informed decisions about how much equity to give or receive, and at what price. A valuation can also help determine whether a startup is over or undervalued, and can be useful in negotiating deals or attracting new investors.

11 Bonus

Accelerator

Accelerator

An **accelerator** is a hub where startups are given mentorship, space to work on their ideas, and sometimes seed capital.

Accredited Investor

The SEC (Securities and Exchange Commission) defines an **accredited investor** as, "A natural person with income exceeding $200,000 in each of the two most recent years or joint income with spouse exceeding $300,000 for those years and a reasonable expectation of the same income level in the current year; or a natural person who has an individual net worth, or joint net worth with the person's spouse, that exceeds $1 million at the time of the purchase, excluding the value of the primary residence of such person." In layman's terms, it is a rich individual potentially interested in investing in your company.

Advertorials / Advertainment

Advertorials are paid content that is meant to look and feel like a true story or blog post. Companies are turning to these because display ad pricing has become less effective and viewers have become immune to them.

Acquisition

An **acquisition** is when one company or investment group buys another company.

Bootstrapping

One of the most common expressions in the startup world. A lot of people will quote "the Three Fs": Friends, Family, and Fools. These channels are often where you get your first cash to get things going. If you are using very little capital and proving your hypothesis, you are successfully **bootstrapping.**

B2B

B2B

B2B means you offering a "Business To Business" product or service to other companies.

B2C

B2C

B2C means you offer your products or services to other consumers (Business To Consumer).

Bubble

Bubble

A **bubble** describes a moment in an economic cycle where an industry or company does not realize that it might be overvalued and over-inflated. When a "tech bubble" bursts, it means that a lot of startups go bust and investors lose their money.

Burn Rate

Burn Rate

Burn rate describes how fast you go through your cash. The majority of startups lose before they break even and then make a profit.

Cash Flow Positive

Cash flow positive

Cash flow positive is accountant speak meaning that more money is coming in than going out. When you deduct your expenses from your earnings, you have a positive amount in your bank account. Staying in the black, especially when you are self-funded is the name of the game!

Churn Rate

churn rate

The **churn rate** is the annual percentage rate at which customers stop subscribing to a service or employees leave a job.

Cliff

A **cliff** usually applies to vesting schedules (shares given to employees over time). Cliffs can be a device for the CEO to fire employees or let them leave without giving them stock within a limited period of time (usually 1 year). There are horror stories from Silicon Valley about early employees being cut just before they get to receive their equity stake. Cliffs are also used on CEOs by investors to make sure the CEO sticks around after getting the cash.

Copyright

Copyright

Usually used in the creative industry, **copyrights** protect your music, art and film. It allows the creator to have exclusive rights for its use and distribution.

Cottage Business / Cottage Industry

Cottage Business / Cottage Industry

A **cottage business** is one that is never going to make millions or scale but can be a nice lifestyle business.

Crowdfunding

Crowdfunding

Crowdfunding is the act of using a site like Kickstarterto get a tribe of early fans together to give you money to help you get your product/site launched. You keep 100% of your company and only give away a % the total you raise to the crowdfunding portal.

Crowdsourcing

Crowdsourcing

Crowdsourcing is getting information for free from people on the internet or using a survey.

Deck (aka Pitch Deck)

Deck (aka Pitch Deck)

A **deck** is a presentation that covers all aspects of your business in a succinct and exciting way. If you ever need inspiration for a good deck, check out how Elon Musk uses his to demonstrate the TESLA Powerwall.

Demographic

Demographic

The demographic is an expression that is frequently used in marketing to describe the age, gender, income, schooling, and occupation of your ideal customers.

Digital Nomad

Digital Nomad

A **digital nomad** is typically a web or app developer who travels the world while coding. There are forecasted to be $1 billion digital nomads by 2035.

Disruptive Technology

Disruptive technology

Disruptive technology is any tech that takes an industry, forces consumers to think differently, and then adopts that technology as the new norm. Examples include Uber, Lyft, Airbnb, and JetSmarter.

Early Adopters

Early Adopters

Early adopters are the first users of your product. They will typically be key influencers and active on social media. They will give you your most honest and sometimes overly direct feedback. If you can identify these people effectively and have them interacting with your startup from an early stage, you can get lots of free exposure.

Ecosystem

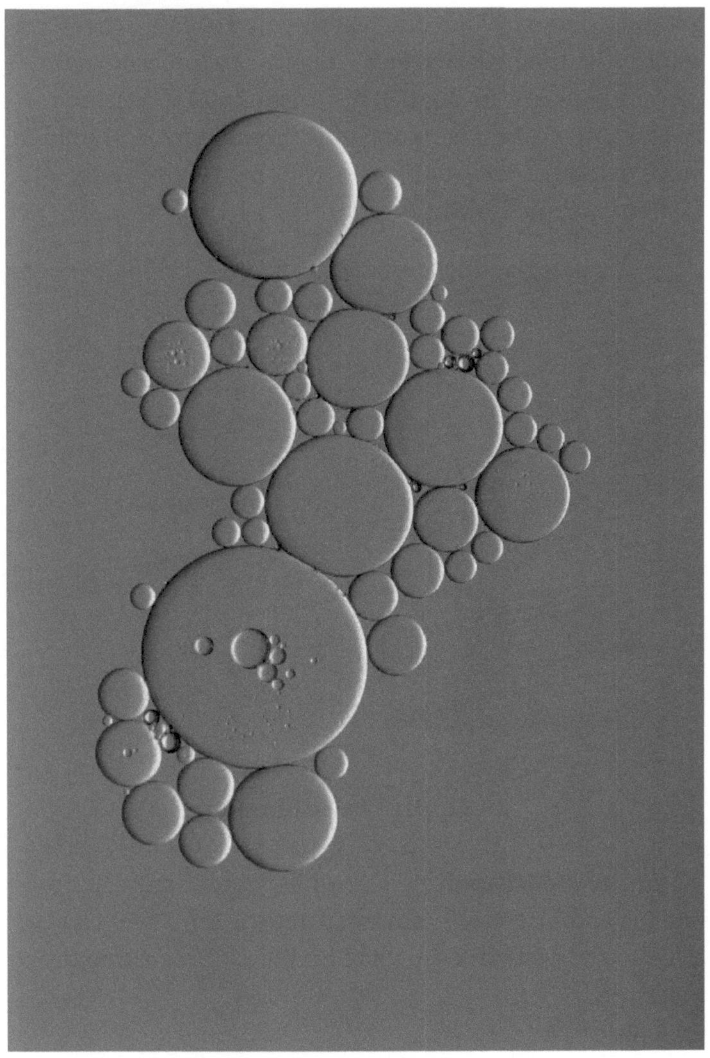

Ecosystem

As with an ecosystem in nature, a startup **ecosystem** has its food chain. There are the hunters, the herd, and the bottom feeders. Work out where you are and where you want to be then get involved in your startup ecosystem. If the city you are in doesn't have incubators, accelerators, co-working spaces, mentors, and investors, you should a). move to another city, or b). start your own ecosystem.

Equity Crowdfunding

Equity Crowdfunding

Equity crowdfunding is just like regular crowdfunding but instead of getting money in return for a fee, you pay a fee to the crowdfunding site and a % of the company to investors.

Evangelist

Evangelist

An **evangelist** is someone inside your organization who is your number one fan. They love your company so much that they often go above and beyond their expected role to help promote your company. If you find an evangelist, hire them!

Exit Strategy

Exit Strategy

The exit strategy is how you plan to sell your company to give you and your investors a return on their investment. This ranges depending on the industry but a standard multiple with technology investments seems to be 10x.

FMA (First Mover Advantage)

FMA (First Mover Advantage)

The first to market is not always the first to capitalize on the industry. One reason for this is that it can cost a fortune to educate potential users or customers. That said, if you are a company like Disney, you lead, and by innovating you stay ahead of the pack. This is called the **first mover advantage.**

Freemium

Freemium

A **freemium** approach is when giving your basic product away for free and then try to upsell other features to your customers. It is a common and proven technique to acquire more users.

Gamify

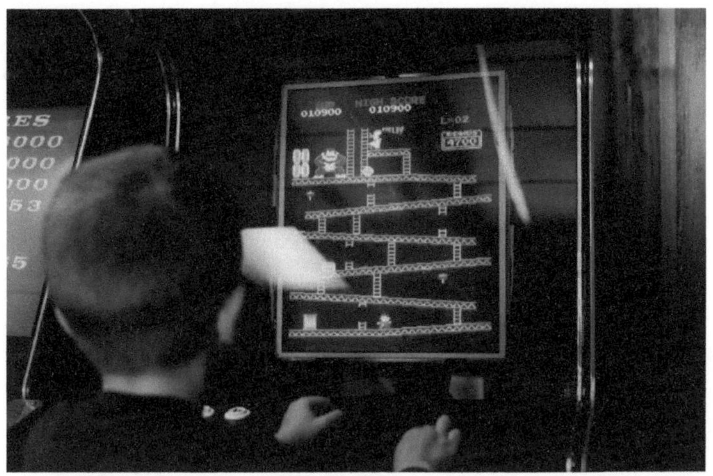

Gamify

If you **gamify** something, you add a game layer to your product that encourages people to use it with rewards of various kinds. See Foursquare and how they used virtual badges and the "Mayor" badge to encourage people to use their app.

Growth Hacking

Growth Hacking

Growth Hacking was a term first used by Sean Ellis (Dropbox) to describe a marketing technique that focuses on quickly finding scalable growth through non-traditional and inexpensive tactics such as the use of social media. Other companies that have effectively used this technique are Airbnb and Founder.

Hacking

Growth Hacking

Hacking is using your computer science degree and your entrepreneurial flare to create disruptive technology. Look out for "hacker houses" and "hackathons" if you want to join the tech community.

Hockey Stick

Hockey Stick

The hockey stick is an expression used by investors to describe the shape of the growth curve they want to see in businesses they invest in. They want to see their startups grow quickly and at least double sales every year.

IP (Intellectual Property)

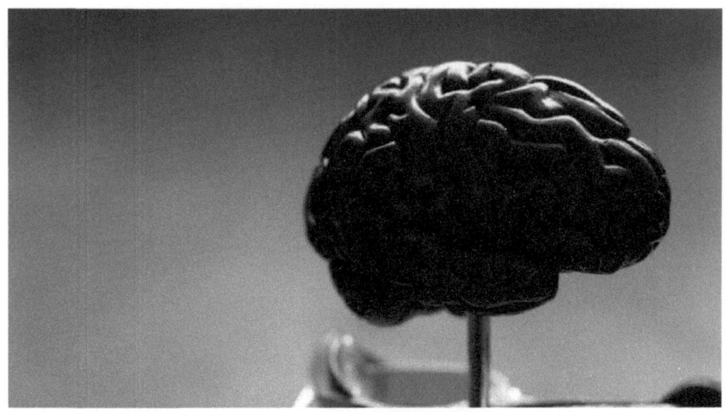

IP (Intellectual Property)

Intellectual property covers patents, trademarks, and copyrights. It is a good way to protect your "secret sauce". Generally, I remember them like this:

Patents — the DNA of your product. They are typically used to protect your design.

Trademarks — they are used to protect your brand and depending on which one you register, you can add a "™ " or "®" (Registered Trademark) next to your logo.

Copyright — they are used to protect your creative content (like film, music or art) and it allows you to use a "©" symbol on your content.

Iterate

Iterate

Iterate means to try something, refine it, try again, and keep trying using small steps until successful.

Laggards

Laggards

Laggards are users who join your movement or buy from you much later than other customers.

Launch

A **launch** is when you start a company, website, or app. It is the euphoric moment when you feel that the blood, sweat, and tears were worth it. Companies can either have a "soft launch" (minimal press exposure and staying in beta) or celebrate with a "launch party" which can be a major startup events like CES or Startup Week.

Lean Startup

Lean Startup

A **lean startup** is one that has been launched with as little startup capital as possible while getting data that can be used to improve the product. Speed is the key factor here.

Leverage

Leverage

Leverage is using something to accelerate your growth or success. This is often found in the form of technology or partnerships. Think about a Formula One car getting in the slipstream of a car in front of it so it can be catapulted out at a faster speed and overtake it.

Loss Leader Pricing

Loss Leader Pricing

Loss leader pricing is using deliberately low pricing to gain market share. The key here is to tempt your users with the low price or free offer and once you have acquired them, focus on how you can get repeat business from them.

Low Hanging Fruit

Low Hanging Fruit

Low-hanging fruits are things that can be identified to quickly bring cash in the door. Your first customers will keep you afloat and help you get to your cash cows (reliable and consistent revenue generators) and whales (your accounts that make you big bucks).

LTV / CAC Ratio (Lifetime Value / Cost to Acquire Customer)

LTV / CAC Ratio (Lifetime Value / Cost to Acquire Customer)

This compares the **lifetime value** (LTV) of a customer to the **cost to acquire** them (CAC). A good explanation is given by Ande Lyons.

Market Penetration

You will frequently hear the line "how much of the pie are you trying to get?" from investors. What they mean is how much market share will be yours and in what time period? They want to know what your **market penetration** will be.

Merger

Merger

A **merger** is when two companies join forces and become a joint entity.

Monetize

Monetize

How you make money. Do you sell online, offer consulting services, or sell face-to-face? Without a way to **monetize**, most businesses die. The only exceptions are well-funded tech startups where a bet has been made that the site will get enough users so that a monetization strategy can eventually be executed. This is highly risky but the reward is high.

MVP (Minimum Viable Product)

A **minimum viable product** is the simplest form of your product. This can be used to attract Beta users/early adopters or to pitch for funding.

OPM (Other People's Money)

OPM (Other People's Money)

When you use **other people's money** to fund your startup, you use the "Three Fs": friends, family or fools.

Pivot

Pivot

A change in direction as a company. This is a key moment in the life of a startup and can make or break it. A well-known **pivot** is when Fab went from being a gay social network to being an e-commerce curator.

PR (Public Relations)

PR (Public Relations)

It is useful to have a **public relations** firm if you have a marketing budget. If not, you might want to spend some time reaching out to your local and industry-specific publications. The best press is free press!

Ramen Profitable

Ramen Profitable

Ramen profitable is an expression frequently used by Paul Graham of Y Combinator, it means you are making just enough money to be able to pay for basic living expenses.

Responsive Design

Responsive Design

Responsive design is an integral part of a website that has been built to function well across all devices. Your site might appear completely different on the web compared to mobile but as long as your end users are always considered, you will be fine.

ROI (Return On Investment)

ROI (Return On Investment)

When an investor puts money into a company, he wants to know what he will get out. This is called the **return on investment**. The investor(s) will also want to know how long it will take to get their ROI?

Runway

Runway

A **runway** describes how long your cash will last and when you think it will run out. The key here is knowing when to start pitching for investment so you can time it to come in before you run out of cash.

Scaleable

Scaleable

How big your business can grow, how much market demand you have and which markets you can grow into. A common question from investors is, "How **scaleable** is this opportunity?" If you cannot scale, you might fall under the "Cottage Industry" or "Lifestyle Business" category.

Serial Entrepreneur

Serial Entrepreneur

A **serial entrepreneur** is someone who launches a number of businesses either simultaneously or one after another. And if they launch something you can eat for breakfast, they are a serial cereal entrepreneur!

Sweat Equity

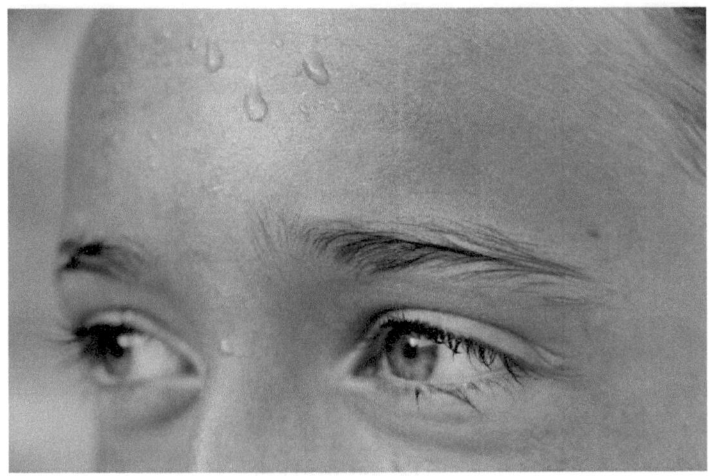

Sweat Equity

Sweat equity is when you give shares of your company to early employees or contractors in place of cash. This is very common in the startup world before funding arrives. If you take a chance with a startup, your shares might become lucrative when the company sells.

Target Market

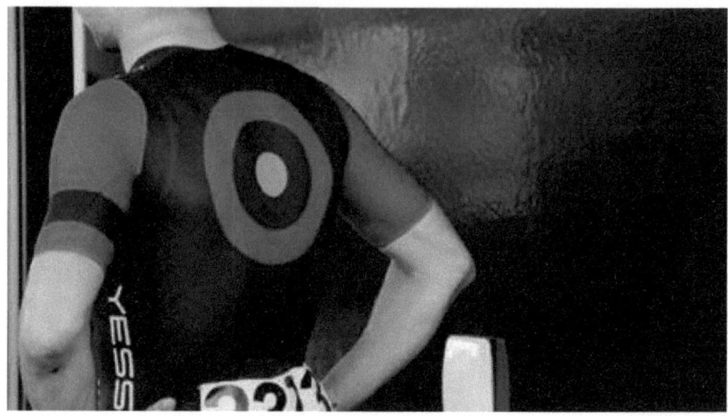

Target Market

You need to identify who will be buying your product, their demographic and their location. Once you have this data, you have your **target market.**

Term Sheet

Term Sheet

When an investor makes you an offer to invest in your company, the **term sheet** is a document that outlines what they will get for what they put in — including % ownership and voting rights.

Traction

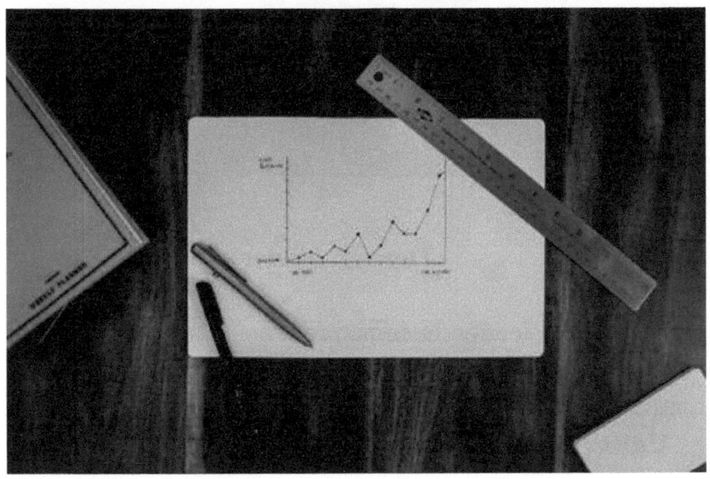

Traction

Traction is proof that your executive summary (hypothesis) is working. People are actually buying your product or using your service. This is one of the most exciting times in a startup!

Thought Leader

Thought Leader

A **thought leader** is someone who is seen as being a leader in their field, is invited to speak at conferences, and has probably published at least one book.

Unicorn

Unicorn

A **unicorn** is a company that gets a $1 billion valuation. As with most unicorns (like the ones that busk at subway stations), they are extremely rare.

UI (User Interface)

UI (User Interface)

The **user interface** is how the user and computer system interact. If you hear someone say “they need a new UI guy”, it means the user has difficulty operating the product.

Valuation

Valuation

A **valuation** describes what your company is being valued at. "Pre-money valuation" is the value before you take investors' cash. "Post-money valuation" is that amount plus the investment put in. I would definitely recommend speaking to other Founders and accountants about how to accurately get a valuation for your business. If you are selling your company, typically the Buyer is trying to get the lowest valuation so he can acquire your business for cheap. As the Seller, you have to establish a fair valuation (typically a fair multiple for your industry) with a slight margin. Example: if your net profit at the end of the year is $100k, it might be 2–3x ($200–300k) if the company has plateaued. If it is a tech business with rapid growth, the multiple might be 10x ($1 million).

Value Proposition

The value proposition is what makes your business uniquely attractive. Also known as USPs (Unique Selling Points).

VC (Venture Capitalist)

VC (Venture Capitalist)

If you are an entrepreneur, you might think of **VC**s as corporate, evil money hungry vultures. Some of them are and will screw you! Do your diligence on them (as they would on you and your startup) and make sure you have investors who align with your beliefs. Do they want to change the world like you (get them on board) or just want a steady return (yawn).

Visionary

Visionary

A **visionary** is an entrepreneur who sees the change in the world before it has happened. Many say that these people have the ability to peer into their crystal balls and then develop something that we will eventually need. Famous examples of visionaries include Richard Branson, Elon Musk, and Walt Disney.

Thank You

Thank you for reading this book on Startup jargon. We hope it has provided you with a helpful introduction to the most common terms and concepts used in the startup world.

Starting and growing a business can be a challenging journey, but understanding the language and concepts of the industry can help make the process smoother and more manageable.

Remember that these jargons are not only important for understanding the startup world, but it can also help you communicate your ideas and plans effectively to others.

We wish you the best of luck on your entrepreneurial journey, and we hope that this book has been a useful resource for you.

Sincerely,
Akshay Raj

9 798889 862956

Printed by Libri Plureos GmbH in Hamburg, Germany